Mexican Details

Mexican Details

Karen Witynski
Joe P. Carr

Photography by Karen Witynski

Gibbs Smith, Publisher
Salt Lake City

For Addison

First Paperback Edition

10 09 08 07 06   5 4 3 2 1

Published by
Gibbs Smith, Publisher
P.O. Box 667
Layton, UT 84041

Orders (1-800) 748-5439
www.gibbs-smith.com

Designed by CN Design
Printed in China

Library of Congress Cataloging-in-Publication Data

Witynski, Karen, 1960-
  Mexican details / Karen Witynski and Joe P. Carr.— 1st ed.
    p. cm.
  ISBN 1-58685-032-6 (hb); 1-4236-0025-8 (pbk)
1. Decorative arts—Mexico. 2. Ethnic art in interior decoration.
3. Decorative arts—Conservation and restoration—Texas—Austin.
I. Carr, Joe P., 1942- II. Title.
NK844 .W55 2003
745'.0972—dc21
                            2002012791

We would like to acknowledge AEROMEXICO for their special support with air transportation during research trips to Mexico.

Front Jacket: Old Mexican dance masks are paired with an antique, hand-painted Mexican trunk to create a colorful statement. Collection of the authors, Karen Witynski and Joe P. Carr.

Half-Title & Title Page: Hacienda Chan Poxilá's colorful portal features elegant iron plant stands and a Mayan cross displayed atop a stone, Yucatán, Mexico.

Back Jacket: A Spanish-style table designed by Joe Carr anchors the dramatic comedor (dining room) at Hacienda Petac, Yucatán, Mexico.

CONTENTS

A hacienda machinery mold hangs above a Mexican chip-carved bench and coffee table adapted from a Mayan mesa de moler (grinding table), Joe P. Carr Design.

THROUGH A PERIOD OF TWO AND A HALF DECADES WORKING AS DESIGNERS AND

GALLERY OWNERS SPECIALIZING IN MEXICAN COLONIAL ANTIQUES AND ARCHITEC-

TURAL ELEMENTS, IT IS OUR CAPTIVATION WITH THE RICHNESS OF THE MEXICAN CUL-

TURE AND ITS HANDCRAFTED DESIGN DETAILS THAT HAS BEEN OUR COMPASS. A DEEP

INTEREST IN THE WORLD OF MEXICAN FURNISHINGS AND ITS INFLUENCE ON TODAY'S

CONTEMPORARY INTERIORS HAS LED US ON COUNTLESS FASCINATING DESIGN

INTRODUCTION

PILGRIMAGES THROUGHOUT MEXICO. OUR EARLY TRAVELS FOCUSED ON THE COLLEC-

TION OF COUNTRY AND COLONIAL FURNITURE, DOORS AND DECORATIVE ACCENTS,

PIECES WE OFTEN UNCOVERED IN OFF-THE-BEATEN-TRACK SALVAGE YARDS, WARE-

HOUSES AND DUSTY ANTIQUE SHOPS. TODAY, OUR MEXICAN BUYING TRIPS CONTINUE

AS WE SEEK ANTIQUES FOR OUR DESIGN CLIENTS AND OUR GALLERY, JOE P. CARR

DESIGN IN AUSTIN, TEXAS. THE CULMINATION OF OUR RESEARCH AND TRAVELS HAS

BEEN A SERIES OF SIX BOOKS AND A TWO-YEAR HACIENDA RESTORATION PROJECT.

Lured by the character-rich details and deeply patinated surfaces we were encountering, we have continued our quest to discover Mexican elements whose distinguishing marks resonate with beauty and ingenuity. From hand-hewn tortilla tables and chip-carved benches, to painted trunks and carved-stone moldings, the soulful nature of Mexican design abounds. Intricately woven textiles, hand-carved masks and finely crafted ceramics are other beautiful examples of elements whose peculiar details are reflections of the hands that made them.

An old hand-carved coffee mortar displays shapely gourds in a contemporary setting. Painting by Mara Beth Witynski.

Opposite: No longer in use, old coffee mortars are retrieved from a Mexican warehouse by co-author Joe Carr. Cleaned and waxed, these hand-carved vessels become unique, sculptural design accents.

Christened by our experiences meeting innovative village craftsmen, carpenters and architects, we soon found ourselves further immersed in photographing the nuances of Mexican design. From unique dovetail joinery on furniture and hand-wrought iron hardware, to mesmerizing chinked-stone wall patterns, stencils and stucco finishes, we found the variety of local innovations astounding.

Documenting the origins of Mexican furnishings, objects and architectural details and transporting old-world treasures back to life through restoration and new adaptation has brought us great pleasure. Through our gallery business we have revived old tables, doors and culinary antiques in our workshop, then replaced them in U.S. homes, prominent hotels, restaurants and specialty stores.

An antique door and contemporary iron base combine to create a unique custom table.

Opposite: An antique mesquite door becomes a unique headboard with the addition of wrought-iron finials. Joe P. Carr Design, Austin, Texas.

Red gladiolas in an old carved-stone water filter contrast beautifully with the richly painted walls of Hacienda Petac's private chapel.

Our continual focus is on introducing creative reuse of once-utilitarian elements, as well as offering custom tables fashioned from reclaimed Mexican woods. We have turned cypress doors with old *clavos horizontal* into unique console tables, seen stone water filters flower as planters, and upended rustic corral gates to mount into headboards. Many storage trunks, long separated from their original wooden bases, are returned to function with custom wrought-iron bases. Even unassuming objects, many no longer in use, beautifully ornament their surroundings with wit and charm when placed in new contexts. For example, old dough bowls, mortars and stone *pilas* were creatively displayed in Banana Republic stores as special old-world accents. Old lockplates, keys or hacienda machine molds also make a vibrant mosaic in multiple wall groupings.

Architectural elements—including doors, shutters, gates, wrought-iron grilles and pediments—were some of the first items we found that most easily adapted to functional pieces. With the addition of iron finials and a base, a pair of doors with only one useable side became a headboard. Odd-sized shutters, replete with their intact hardware, easily made the transition to coffee tables. A timeworn balcony balustrade was turned vertically to become a base for a stone-topped table. Thick wooden corbels once used to support old *vigas* (beams) in colonial homes and haciendas have now found many new uses—we have adapted them to wall-mounted console tables, shelves and matching night-stands. More casual innovations have also seen old corbels used as support elements for antique trunks and stone vessels on hacienda *portales*.

The ubiquitous Mexican table—through its life in the home, workplace, church and market—reveals many variations: the brightly painted turned legs of kitchen tables; the ranch table's square, A-frame legs; the simple, tapered legs of market prep tables; the home altar tables marked by candle-wax burns; and the carved baroque-style legs of colonial tables.

Having seen and examined these types and hundreds of other Mexican tables, our observations have allowed us to distinguish between styles, recognize Spanish-influenced design characteristics, and develop a sense of how particular tables can be incorporated into contemporary interiors. Inspired by many of the fine examples we have found over the years, we have established our own Mexican Style line of custom tables.

Mexican Details was born in part from our many years of traveling for our gallery and the research we have done on our previous five books. For our first volume, *Mexican Country Style*, we documented rare examples of both country furniture and architectural elements. With *The New Hacienda*, we went to newly restored grand estates resplendent with hand-hewn beams, massive doors and colonial furniture. *Casa Adobe*, the third volume, brought us closer to the golden glow of mud-plastered walls and the contoured corners of adobe *nichos*. *Adobe Details* revealed fascinating collections of found objects, *santos* and devotional art expressions that often adorn adobe homes. In *Casa Yucatán*, we shared our fascination with colonial courtyards, artful water features and the ever present blending of Spanish and Maya design influences.

It is in this book, *Mexican Details*, that we magnify the elegance of many of those handcrafted design details that grace our earlier books. The contacts we have made with leading architects and preservationists in the field of colonial restoration, in addition to allowing us to discover rare examples of furniture and objects, have provided a unique education in regional construction techniques and the historical influences of colors and textures.

hacienda petac

Right: A Spanish-style table designed by Joe Carr anchors Hacienda Petac's dramatic comedor *(dining room).*

Opposite: Spacious guest rooms, housed in Hacienda Petac's former casa de máquina, *feature twenty-two-foot ceilings accented by colorful walls. An original support bracket was adapted into a unique light sconce by architect Salvador Reyes Ríos.*

In our endeavors of rescuing and restoring Mexican elements and working with pioneers in the field, we found ourselves drawn to the idea of taking our research one step farther into experience. Following the completion of *The New Hacienda* in 1999, we discovered, then very quickly became enamored with, an eighteenth-century colonial hacienda named Petac, graceful in its decay and ripe with restorative possibilities. The experience of working on the restoration and design of this property has been, perhaps, a predictable step in our creative evolution and research of Mexican design, as well as a uniquely exciting and educational foray into the finer nuances of Yucatecan architecture and building methods.

An arched wall heightens
the drama of Hacienda
Petac's grand-scale
bathroom, and provides
privacy for a W.C. and
separate shower.

Opposite: An old stone
metate (grinding stone)
becomes a textural
surface on which to
display hand towels.

A sculptural ménsula
(architectural bracket)
postures beneath
Goldenrain Tree
Pods, a painting by
Judith M. Simpson.

Opposite: In Hacienda
Petac's restored casa
de máquina, a
partially exposed
section of art graffiti
has been preserved and
framed as a relic of
the building's past—
and a reminder of the
worker's playfulness.

ménsula

COLOR

Yucatán architecture
displays an innovative
use of texture and color.

& TEXTURE

FOR CENTURIES, MEXICO'S COMPELLING COLORS HAVE PROVIDED A VIBRANT AND POWERFUL PRESENCE TO ITS ARCHITECTURE AND TRADITIONAL ARTS. BEGINNING WITH THE PRE-HISPANIC CIVILIZATION'S BOLDLY PAINTED PYRAMIDS, COLORFUL MURALS AND STUCCO ORNAMENTS, THROUGH THE SPANISH COLONIAL HACIENDAS AWASH IN DEEP REDS, OCHRES OR BLUES, TO TODAY'S MODERN HOUSES SPLASHED IN WATERMELON PINK AND PISTACHIO GREEN, THE COLOR LEGACY IN MEXICO IS LONG AND RICH.

Left: Colorful concrete floor tile complements the richly painted walls of this colonial hacienda. A rebozo is draped over an old hammock hook.

Opposite: Lime-based paint brightens up Yucatán's stone-chinked and plastered walls.

Arresting color combinations found in Mexico's traditional arts engage the senses and enrich rooms with energy. From dazzling, beaded Huichol gourds and yarn paintings to Maya embroidered textiles, ceremonial masks and richly glazed ceramics, the artistic expressions reflect the symbolism and energy attached to the medium of color.

An essential form of self-expression, color has long been used to represent spiritual beliefs and cultural traditions. In fact, color and its attendant symbolism remain pivotal to the Mayas' view of their cosmos. A color diamond signifying the physical world was at the core of their view of the universe. White, yellow, red and black each had a place corresponding to the four cardinal directions of north, south, east and west, along the path of the sun.

Red *(chac)* represents east, the dawn, blood of sacrifice and rain; yellow *(kan)* represents south, life-sustaining corn and midday sun; white *(sak)* represents north, cold and change; black *(ek)* represents west, destruction and night. At the center of the Mayas' multilayered cosmos is the sacred *yaxché*, or ceiba tree. Awash in blue-green *(yax)*, the ceiba's color and position represents many life-giving elements, including water.

Rich tones of ochre are a favored color throughout Yucatán architecture.

Opposite, top: Old decorative stencils enliven hacienda walls in the Yucatán. Bottom: An outlined window adds drama to a rich ochre wall.

Mediterranean blue and golden walls are accented with decorative stencils along the inviting corridors at Medio Mundo Hotel in Yucatán. The custom stencil was adapted from the design of a ceramic plate made during the Ottoman Empire in Turkey.

The Medio Mundo owners added unique texture to the floors by designing the tiles to look like classic Moorish rugs.

The colors used on pre-Hispanic structures and sculptures were natural pigments obtained from mineral and vegetal sources. These ancient colored pigments have lasted centuries, as evidenced by many recently discovered murals in jungle temples. Bonampak, in Chiapas, reveals still-brilliant colors, including the mysterious Maya blue. According to architect Eugene Logan Wagner, this sacred blue was the color most difficult to obtain, and its exact origins were unknown until recently. In 2000, Dr. Miguel José Yacamán, a Mexican nuclear physicist, discerned that in addition to indigo (the plant source), one of the ingredients used to create the blue pigment was a special clay found in the Sacalum region of the Yucatán. In ancient times, this clay was mixed with indigo and heated to 150 degrees centigrade to produce palygorskite crystals in the paint to form a super-lattice. Dr. Wagner adds that different clays from various regions account for the many shades of Maya blue that have survived.

Maya blue differs from any blue ever identified on ancient or medieval paintings from Europe or Asia, as it is not based on copper or ground lapis lazuli or lazulite, common in European and Asian paintings. Currently a professor at the University of Texas, Dr. Yacamán is also working with Dr. Wagner to produce the Maya blue pigment for artistic applications in residential projects.

Reds were obtained predominately from minerals or dirt, including cinnabar and hematite. The cochineal beetle was the principal animal source of red. Ochre, a hydrated iron oxide, provided yellow tones, black was created from carbon, white from calcite found in limestone, and purple tones were obtained from particular ocean shells. Agglutinates and water sealants, essential substances used in the sealing of walls and water receptacles, were also derived from natural resources. In the Yucatán, boiled pixoy leaves were used, and the prickly pear cactus, predominant in other regions, was another source for sealants.

A colonial stucco detail accents this Yucatán hacienda window.

Opposite: A colonial façade features a decorative stucco design and stone-chinked walls, Yucatán, Mexico.

In Mexican architecture, interior walls bathed in vibrant hues are given texture with the addition of colonial-style stencil patterns or wainscots in contrasting colors. Many exterior stone walls, stuccoed and painted with traditional lime-based recipes, feature ornate stucco details around doors and windows and stone-chinked surface patterns. Called *rajueleado*, this masterful stone-chinking tradition reinforces stuccoed surfaces and adds textural dimension and depth to walls.

Adding drama to this Yucatán home is an intricately chinked limestone wall. Designed by architect Alvaro Ponce.

Opposite: A carved-stone door surround adds old-world texture to the entrance of this contemporary Yucatán residence. Designed by architect Alvaro Ponce.

The natural hues found in earth's clay, stone and fibers are also important in Mexican design, counterbalancing its palette of strong colors. From the stark whites of intricately chinked limestone walls and earthy tones of bamboo-brush columns to the rich browns of hand-hewn wooden ceiling beams, the textures of nature's materials contribute an elegant simplicity.

Elegantly painted door surrounds add color and texture to this colonial hacienda.

Opposite: Hacienda Chan Poxilá's blue doors are accented in white against colorfully painted walls. Designed by Alejandro Patrón.

Today's architects and preservationists working in Mexico continue to herald the benefits of natural color pigments, lime-based paints and stucco finishes. In the Yucatán, architect Salvador Reyes Ríos is an avid promoter of using these traditional recipes in his many architectural projects. As lime-based paints and stuccoes are compatible with stone walls, *cal* (lime)-based recipes encourage walls to "breathe," allowing moisture to escape without damaging painted surfaces. Natural paint pigments are also highly favored, as they are more resistant to ultraviolet light, making them more lightfast than synthetic paints.

Richly painted walls and a bamboo ramada *create an inviting* portal *at Hacienda Xcanatún, Yucatán.*

Opposite: A vibrant wall fountain at Casa del Panadero features a kancab *finish.*

A brightly tiled kitchen counter at Hacienda San Gabriel de las Palmas, Morelos.

MEXICAN COCINAS (KITCHENS) ATTRACT
WITH THEIR WARMTH, AROMAS, HUMMING
ACTIVITY AND CHERISHED IMPLEMENTS

COCINAS

THAT EXUDE TIME-HONORED TRADITIONS.
IN TODAY'S MEXICAN COCINAS, COLORFUL
BOLD WALLS AND BRIGHTLY PATTERNED
AZULEJOS (TILES) CONTINUE AS POPULAR
DESIGN ELEMENTS, JUST AS THEY DID IN
THE CENTURIES-OLD CONVENT KITCHENS
OF PUEBLA. IN ADDITION TO THE MEXICAN
KITCHENS FOUND IN COLONIAL HOMES
AND HACIENDAS, THE CONTEMPORARY

MEXICAN KITCHEN HAS EVOLVED WITH FRESH INTERPRETATIONS OF OLD AND NEW THAT CONTINUE TO ECHO THE SPIRIT OF MEXICO'S CULINARY TRADITIONS. THIS INNOVATIVE MIXTURE COMBINES ALL THE FAMILIAR ELEMENTS—HAND-PAINTED TALAVERA-STYLE TILES, RUSTIC WOODEN TABLES, AND EVERYDAY UTILITARIAN OBJECTS—WITH MODERN FIXTURES AND APPLIANCES THAT WORK ALONGSIDE OLD-WORLD ELEMENTS.

A brightly painted
Mexican sideboard adds
charm to a well-equipped
kitchen. Collection of
Barbara Windom and
Victor di Suvero.

Opposite, left: An antique
sideboard from Puebla
displays colorful ceramics
in the dining room of
Barbara Windom and
Victor di Suvero's New
Mexico home. Right: A
heart-shaped Mexican
milking stool.

Right: Old ceramic pitcher with appliquéd design details.

Opposite and below: An innovative use of color and tile creates a playful mood in this kitchen designed by Josefina Larraín.

In addition to tiled counters and large venting hoods, kitchens today often mix natural, traditional materials with contemporary fixtures and highly functional polished and colored concrete surfaces. Modern stovetops rest on old-style counters, providing contrast and convenience, and brightly painted old *trasteros* (freestanding cupboards) stand across from sub-zero refrigerators.

The kitchen at Casa Reyes-Larraín in Mérida, Yucatán, is an excellent example of a Mexican Colonial-style *cocina* that resonates beauty and function through its mix of natural, traditional materials and contemporary design. Designed by architect Salvador Reyes Ríos and designer Josefina Larraín, the kitchen features a fourteen-foot-high venting hood that is traditional in its shape, yet its elongated proportion and bold blue color make a strong contemporary statement. Created on-site with white cement and lime-based paint, the hood features a unique bas-relief decoration on its lower edge, inspired by a French cement-tile pattern. This pattern, first transferred to a handmade wooden mold, was carefully stamped onto the cement surface while it was still fresh.

Below on the counter front, the innovative arrangement of Mexican tiles is a playful combination of patterns. The polished cement counter was colored to match the small 4 x 4-inch handmade tiles made in the state of Guanajuato. At one end of the kitchen, a bold splash of deep blue marks the back wall of a traditional-style *alacena* (built-in wall cabinet). Large hollowed gourds, often used in early kitchens to keep freshly made tortillas warm, now hold flowers in their rounded, organic shapes.

Modern fixtures blend with traditional Talavera tile at Casa Teresa Larraín in Mérida, Yucatán. Designed by Josefina Larraín.

Opposite: Colorful ceramic platters on display at a market in Michoacán.

An antique repisa
(hanging shelf)
displays glasses above
a hand-carved coffee
mortar at Hacienda
Petac, Yucatán.

Opposite: A wooden
tortilla mold was
intricately carved for
use during festive
occasions. Collection
of Karen Witynski
and Joe Carr.

Above the colorful counter at Casa Teresa Larraín, a modern French faucet contrasts elegantly with the familiar patterns of blue, white and yellow Talavera tiles. Draping from stainless-steel towel racks, traditional hand-woven towels are within easy reach of the basin. In this kitchen designed by Josefina Larraín, the use of traditional tiles, red cedar shelves and a *macedonia* stone counter, in addition to stainless-steel French fixtures and accessories, was a prominent theme in her innovative design.

The Fields' kitchen in Mérida, also designed by Reyes and Larraín, is another example of a *cocina* featuring hand-painted tiles as decorative accents. Amidst the cool tile, colored and polished cement and colored plaster awash in the kitchen, custom-made wooden cabinets add balance and warmth.

The progenitors of many design details found in today's contemporary homes are Mexican restaurants and their colorful kitchens. Decorated with regional furniture, folk art and practical objects, many small family-owned restaurants in Mexican towns are a treasure trove of local elements and intriguing color combinations. Glazed ceramic platters, baskets, grain measure boxes and old scales combine with casual wall displays of regional folk art such as playful woodcarvings, toys, textiles and paintings done on *amate* (handmade bark paper).

Often designed in an open style, the regalia of restaurant kitchens is fully exposed, offering fascinating views of deep horseshoe-shaped counters where preparations are in full swing: tortilla presses are in constant use and giant-sized wooden spoons stir *caldos* (stews) simmering in large ceramic pots. Guests gather around long wooden tables draped in hand-woven tablecloths, seated on simple backless benches and stools or brightly painted rush-seat chairs.

Culinary antiques that evoke the rhythms of food preparation include old *molcajetes* (small stone mortars), *metates* (grinding stones), *bateas* (wooden dough bowls), sugar molds, cheese presses, and *cazuelas* (earthenware pots) that brim with chocolate whisks. Hand-carved mortars, once used for wheat and coffee, now decoratively display fruit in newly restored hacienda kitchens.

Old *repisas* (hanging shelves) are often decorated with scalloped molding or decorative crests and continue to be popular accents in working kitchens. Candles or matches are easily accessed in the small drawers of many *repisas*, while the shelves are laden with spice jars, small glasses and carved gourd bowls and cups *(jícaras)*. The ornate style of *repisas* from Oaxaca and Puebla feature bright colors and floral motifs, while those from Chihuahua and northern Mexico are typically crafted from natural pine and mesquite.

Colorful walls are decorated with tile and miniature ceramic pots in the dining room of Los Colorines.

Opposite: This old-world cocina *features traditional blue, white and yellow tile, Fundación Robert Brady, Casa de la Torre, Cuernavaca, Mexico.*

49

Providing a solid surface upon which to grind corn with a stone *metate*, the *mesa de moler*, or grinding table, is a unique element popular in the Yucatán that was traditionally used in Maya homes. Carved from one piece of wood, these rustic tables feature flat surfaces with four- to six-inch-thick sides, open ends, and four pegged legs. Used to grind corn into *masa* (dough), the table's height and design works well to accommodate two people working *metates* on each end. Still in use today, these traditional simple tables have made their way into decorative roles in haciendas and contemporary homes. Used in gardens and patios to hold potted plants, they have also been adapted as unique coffee tables and buffet tables at Joe P. Carr Design in Austin, Texas.

Tortilla tables, another frequent sight in rural Maya villages, have also made their way into ranches, residences and upscale restaurants. Crafted from tropical hardwoods, the thick rounded tops are handhewn from a single piece of wood, and range in size from twelve to twenty-four inches in diameter. Used by Maya villagers to pat out tortillas before placing them on the *comal* for cooking, the smooth tops are supported by three pegged legs. The shorter heights allow for a kneeling or sitting position while working.

A glazed ceramic cooking pot rests atop a table made by Joe Carr from an old Maya tortilla tabletop and a new iron base, collection of the Wilkins family. An antique sugar mold poses as a modern sculptural statement.

Opposite: An elegant ceramic pitcher from the state of Puebla features hand-appliquéd leaves and flowers. Joe P. Carr Design, Austin, Texas.

A lush, fern-filled garden designed by Josefina Larraín surrounds a colonial house in Izamal, Yucatán.

Opposite: A bamboo tree house by Yucatán Bamboo perches above the jungle at Hacienda Xixim.

OUTDOOR SPACES FOR RELAXING, DINING OR SLEEPING TAKE THEIR CUE FROM A HOME'S ARCHITECTURE AND LANDSCAPE. OFTEN THE MOST FAVORED "ROOMS" FOR ENTERTAINING, OPEN-AIR SPACES INVITE INTERPLAY WITH NATURE'S ELEMENTS— WATER, AIR AND LIGHT—AND TAKE ADVANTAGE OF GARDEN FEATURES AND FURNISHINGS TO CREATE A COMFORTABLE, WEATHERED LIVING EXPERIENCE. PRINCI-PAL DESIGNS INCLUDE BREEZY PORTALES (COVERED PORCHES), COBBLED COURT-YARDS, TERRACES AND DAYBED PAVILIONS. SHADE-PROVIDING BAMBOO RAMADAS, OR

OUTDOOR LIVING

WOODEN OVERHANGS COMPRISED OF CLOSELY PLACED PARALLEL POLES OR WOOD PIECES, CAN ADD TO SIMPLE PATIOS THE DECORATIVE BENEFIT OF CONVERGING LIGHT AND SHADOW PATTERNS THAT MOVE WITH THE SUN THROUGHOUT THE DAY. THE NATURAL TEXTURES OF BAMBOO, A SUSTAINABLE RESOURCE GROWN BY YUCATÁN BAMBOO ON THE PENINSULA, BLEND SEAMLESSLY IN OUTDOOR SPACES, SHAPED INTO BRUSH COLUMNS, PLANTERS AND CASUAL FURNITURE AND ACCENTS.

The breezy, open-air portal at Hacienda Poxilá is alive with color, comfortable chairs and antiques.

Once-functional relics of everyday working life have been given new lives as cherished design accents in outdoor spaces. Old Maya stone *metates* align tiled courtyards, stone finials nest as garden sculptures, and stone troughs once used for watering livestock are newly planted with water lilies and *lechuga de agua* (water lettuce). Even old wooden corbels, once used to support ceiling beams, take on new functional roles on hacienda *portales* as supports for stone planters or old trunks.

The serene stone courtyard at Casa Reyes-Larraín features a new water garden surrounding an old wellhead. Designed by Josefina Larraín.

Opposite: A bamboo brush column's natural textures add to this courtyard's casual ambience. Column by Yucatán Bamboo, designed by Josefina Larraín.

agua

56

In regions with warm climates, water features are especially vital to outdoor living. Be it a splashing fountain, a trickling aqueduct, or a brightly tiled *pileta* (ground-level basin with faucet and tiled backsplash to protect garden walls and vegetation), the sight and sound of water create a soothing atmosphere and instant rejuvenation. Quieter water features such as small reflecting pools or fishponds add decorative appeal and visual refreshment to outdoor sanctuaries.

Casa Santa Ana's peaceful garden is anchored by a wall fountain, which flows into a canal that recirculates water. Garden design by Josefina Larraín.

In their elegant simplicity, Mexico's outdoor sanctuaries are inspiring today's architects and designers to incorporate water's presence into a variety of architectural environments.

Pages 60–61: The newly restored casa de máquina (machine house) at Hacienda Petac features a unique water fountain that echoes the design of the estate's original stone aqueducts. Fountain design by Salvador Reyes Ríos.

A peaceful poolside setting at Hacienda La Pinka, Yucatán, Mexico.

Opposite: An open-air daybed pavilion at Hacienda Uayamón is a tranquil garden summit. Designed by Salvador Reyes Ríos.

Designed by Alvaro Ponce, this Yucatán home features a tranquil open-air space with an antique stone basin and lush tropical plants.

THE GREAT EXPRESSIONS OF ARTISTRY

FOUND IN MEXICAN RELIGIOUS ELEMENTS

HAVE THEIR ORIGINS IN THE IMPORTANCE

OF DEVOTION WITHIN THE SPANISH

DEVOTIONAL ELEMENTS

CATHOLIC CULTURE. THE WEALTH WITH

WHICH THE CHURCH WAS ENDOWED

DURING THE SPANISH COLONIAL PERIOD

ATTRACTED MANY OF THE PROMINENT

ARTISTS AND CRAFTSMEN OF THE TIME,

Antique Mexican retablo, collection of authors Joe P. Carr and Karen Witynski.

Opposite: A collection of Mexican crosses is displayed beneath an antique wall sconce at Joe P. Carr Design.

santos

WHO CREATED GRANDILOQUENT COLLEC-
TIONS OF SAINTS, CROSSES, PAINTINGS,
OBJECTS AND FURNITURE, INCLUDING
LARGE VESTMENT CHESTS, ALTAR SCREENS
AND TABLES, REFECTORY TABLES, AND
WOODEN NICHOS IN WHICH TO DISPLAY
THE REVERED SAINTS.

On festive occasions, San Gerónimo de Yaxcopoil is on display in the private chapel of Hacienda Yaxcopoil.

Opposite, left: An elegant hacienda sitting room includes a special display of colonial antiques and hand-carved santos, including La Virgen de la Luz, San José and San Antonio.

Opposite, right: La Purísima Concepción, Joe P. Carr Design.

Because of their revered status, many fine examples of devotional elements have survived over the years. Hand-carved and exquisitely painted *bultos* (three-dimensional carved representations of saints), wooden crosses and crucifixes, and *retablos* (two-dimensional paintings of saints) are the principal forms in which devotional art is expressed and which are most commonly seen today.

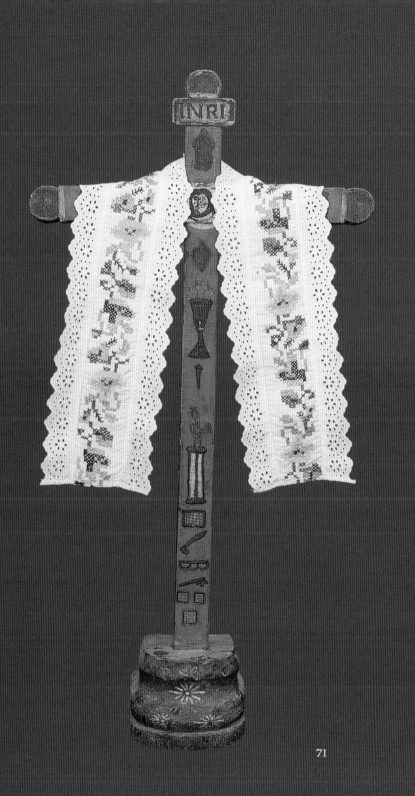

Above: A wooden nicho is decorated with hand-painted flowers and an old Mayan cross.

Left: A traditional hand-painted Mayan cross from the Yucatán.

Opposite: A low stone altar, nicho and antique santo contribute to the heavenly air of Hacienda Petac's tranquil chapel.

Nuestra Señora de la Incarnación, courtesy of Mi Casa Gallery, Austin, Texas.

A collection of antique retablos, courtesy of Mi Casa Gallery, are displayed with an old cross and ceramics atop an antique pine bureau at Joe P. Carr Design. Clockwise from top left: Santa Librata, The Holy Trinity, San Rafael Archangel, Nuestra Señora de la Incarnación, Niño de Atocha print.

A hand-crafted heart exudes simple charm amidst a display of Mexican folk art. Collection of Gloria List.

Throughout Mexico, many colonial churches, convents and private hacienda chapels display museum-quality elements in artfully arranged vignettes that are as fascinating to behold as are the individual elements comprising them. During the principal religious holidays and fiestas, arrangements of fresh flowers, multiple candles, incense holders, silver *milagros* and handmade offerings overflow in homage to the patron saint being celebrated. Small village churches expend no less energy in creating devotional displays: strings of flowers crafted from paper, palm-leaf crosses and straw ornaments decorate interiors, and simple altars are inundated with ceramic candlesticks and images of the Virgin of Guadalupe, the patroness saint of Mexico. Many of these devotional displays reveal a blending of Spanish and Indian imagery and beliefs.

A heart-shaped iron candelabra is aglow with votive candles in the chapel at Hacienda San José Cholul, Yucatán, Mexico.

Mexico's diversity of devotional expression and the way in which religious icons and objects are displayed serve as inspiration for those creating their own home altars or shrines in contemporary residences.

Antique santos *and treasured elements are crowned by decorative iron. Alberto's Continental Patio, Mérida, Yucatán.*

Mater Dolorosa,
Our Lady of Sorrows,
Mi Casa Gallery.

Below: The Virgin
of Guadalupe.

Below: Verónica, El
Rostro Divino, collect-
ion of Joe Carr and
Karen Witynski.

Antique stained-glass window pediments create a unique backdrop for old santos *and family collectibles. Alberto's Continental Patio Restaurant, Yucatán, Mexico.*

An intricately carved and brightly painted *alacena* (wall cabinet) door, Joe P. Carr Design.

Opposite: Gourd carving is a folk art that is popular throughout many regions of Mexico. Collection of Merrick Bonewitz.

HECHO A MANO

THE IMAGINATIVE CRAFTS THAT ARE HECHO A MANO (MADE BY HAND) CHARACTERIZE MEXICO'S RICH ARTISTIC LEGACY. WITH THEIR ROOTS IN PRE-HISPANIC TRADITIONS, TODAY'S NATIVE CRAFTSPEOPLE CONTINUE TO EXPRESS THEIR ARTISTRY IN CLAY, WOOD, STONE, NATURAL FIBERS, TEXTILES AND METALS. CERAMICS, PALM BASKETS, HAND-CARVED MASKS, WOVEN AND

HAND-EMBROIDERED TEXTILES,
PAINTED TOYS AND FANCIFUL
WOODCARVINGS ARE PART OF
THE VAST REPERTOIRE OF MEXI-
CAN HANDCRAFTED ELEMENTS.
ADORNING MEXICO'S BUSTLING
MARKETS AND SHOPS, THESE
CRAFTS ARE TODAY AVAILABLE IN
SPECIALTY STORES AND FOLK ART
GALLERIES AROUND THE WORLD.

Reflecting ancient spiritual beliefs and traditions, mask making is one of Mexico's oldest arts. The masks, worn for ceremonial and religious ritual dances, allowed dancers to be transformed spiritually and psychologically into gods or supernatural forces.

A highly original craft, masks have infinite subtleties that reflect the indigenous traditions and regions in which they are made. Details in their carving, paint and decoration make each one extremely unique. The masks crafted in northwestern Mexico tend to be more primitive and plain, in contrast to those of central and southern Mexico, which are more detailed and colorfully painted. Strands of horsehair are commonly used to create mustaches, eyelashes and hairpieces. In Tlaxcala, masks stare back with beautiful, realistic glass eyes, and those from Guanajuato are often decorated with painted cow horns.

*Mexican dance masks,
collection of Joe Carr
and Karen Witynski.*

*Clockwise from top:
Mask from Sonora,
Mask from Veracruz,
Mask from Michoacán,
Mask from Oaxaca.*

*Center: Mask from
Oaxaca.*

*Opposite: An antique
Mexican mask from
Jalisco. Collection of Joe
Carr and Karen Witynski.*

A golden-yellow glaze decorates this well-crafted ceramic piña pot from Michoacán.

Opposite: Ceramic piña *pots, typical of the traditional styles made in San José del Grazia, Michoacán.*

piña

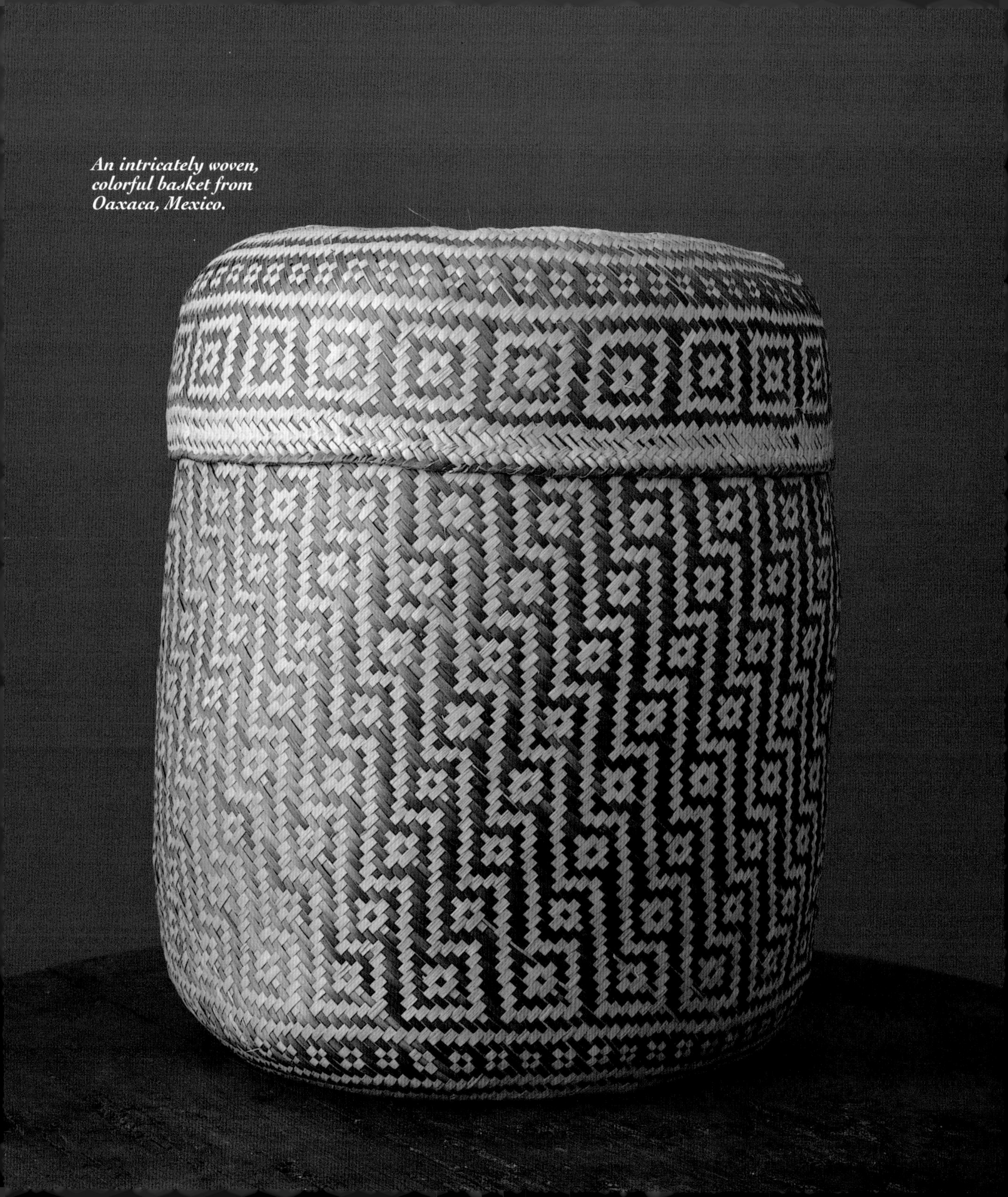

Southern Tepehuan
Indian shoulder bag,
San Francisco
Cayman, Nayarit.
Unique, small Maya
shoulder bag from
the state of Chiapas.

Right: Embroidered
Yucatán huipil.

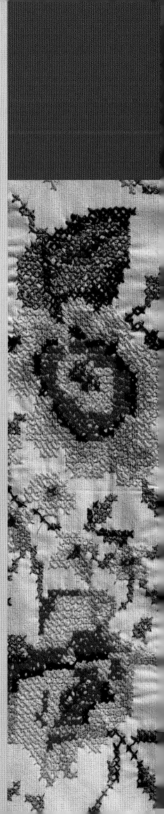

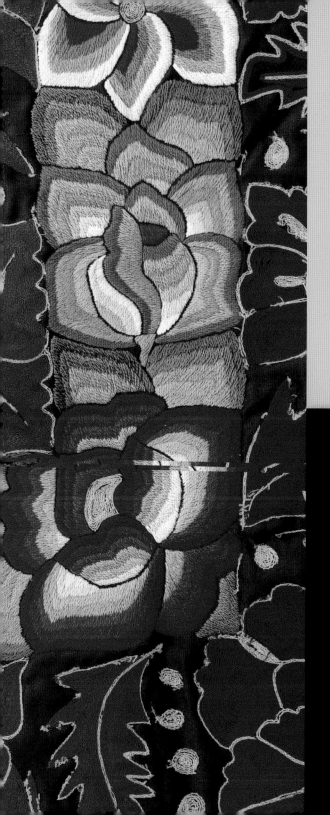

The mask carver's art has survived for centuries, and many exquisite examples of old masks are exhibited in fine museums today. To the true ceremonial dance mask collector, the backside of a mask—with its scores, markings and worn spots—is just as fascinating as its front side.

An embroidered huipil *from the state of Oaxaca, Isthmus of Tehuantepec features colorful flowers, a common motif of this region. Collection of Joe Carr and Karen Witynski.*

Below: Carved wooden folk art skeleton from the state of Oaxaca, Mexico. Collection of Joe Carr and Karen Witynski.

Right: An old skeleton mask crafted for Oaxaca's Day of the Dead celebration.

Opposite: Folk art ceramic merry-go-round crafted by Candelario Medrano.

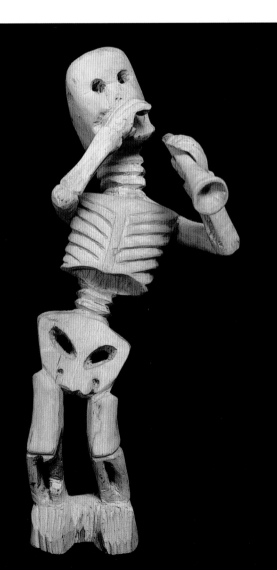

RESOURCES

www.mexicanstyle.com

We invite you to visit our gallery, **Joe P. Carr Design**, for Mexican colonial antiques and architectural elements, including old doors, wrought-iron grilles, ceiling beams and hundred-year-old wood flooring. In addition to antique trunks, benches and harvest tables, we also offer a line of custom "Hacienda" tables featuring reclaimed Mexican hardwoods. Decorative accents include Mexican crosses, *santos*, antique ceramics and black-and-white photography.

Please visit our web site www.mexicanstyle.com for design news and book previews.

Ceramic tamalero pots rest atop a "Mexican Ranch Table" by Joe Carr, Joe P. Carr Design.

AUTHORS' MAILING ADDRESS
JOE P. CARR &
KAREN WITYNSKI
3267 Bee Caves Road #107-181
Austin, TX 78746
(512) 370-9663 tel
(512) 328-2966 fax
www.mexicanstyle.com

AUTHORS' GALLERY
JOE P. CARR DESIGN
3601 Bee Caves Road
at Barton Springs Nursery
Austin, TX 78746
(512) 327-8284

KAREN WITYNSKI
ARCHITECTURAL &
INTERIOR PHOTOGRAPHY
(512) 370-9663 tel
(512) 328-2966 fax

Antique Mexican buffet, Joe P. Carr Design.

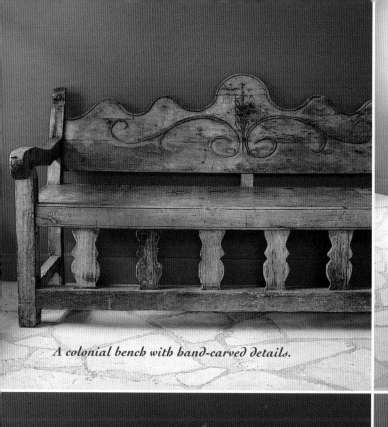

A colonial bench with hand-carved details.

"Hacienda Round Table" by Joe Carr.

"Mérida Table" by Joe Carr, made with antique tiles.

Antique mesquite doors were fashioned into a coffee table by Joe Carr. Collection of Cathy Broussard.

DESIGN SOURCES

featured in this book

Reyes Ríos + Larraín + Konzevik
Restoration, Architecture, Design &
Landscape Studio
Mérida, Yucatán
(999) 923-58-08
reyesrios@prodigy.net.mx

Salvador Reyes Ríos/Josefina Larraín
Furniture Design, Tile Design & Color
Consulting
Mérida, Yucatán
(999) 923-58-08
jlarrain@sureste.com

Alvaro Ponce/Architect
Mérida, Yucatán
(999) 943-30-75
corvina@tponce.com

Alejandro Patrón–Builder/Designer
Mérida, Yucatán
(999) 944-93-79

E. Logan Wagner/Architect
Austin, Texas
(512) 441-9729
Alarife@aol.com

Yucatán Bamboo, Inc.
Houston, Texas
(713) 278-7344
www.yucatanbamboo.com

Joe P. Carr Design
Austin, Texas
(512) 370-9663
www.mexicanstyle.com

Other locations featured in *Mexican Details*:
www.hacienda-sangabriel.com.mx
www.xcanatun.com
www.hotelmediomundo.com
www.luxurycollection.com
www.mexicanstyle.com

A collection of Mexican antiques and custom
tables by Joe Carr are on display at Joe P.
Carr Design, Austin, Texas. Clockwise from
top left: Colonial trunk on stand, antique
market table, old ceramic pitchers, custom
Spanish-style table, custom round table.

Opposite: Colonial antiques on display at
Joe P. Carr Design, Austin, Texas.

Mr. Puppy poses with a colonial trunk at Joe P. Carr Design.